Hello, I am Oliver, your guide on this ex the Web3 realm. My experience in entrepreneurship and investment fuels my commitment to empowering you in the crypto and Web3 field.

As the founder & CEO of StakedX in Dubai, I have witnessed the transformative power of blockchain firsthand, steering through the dynamic waves of the digital economy. My journey has been shaped by roles as a CEO, investor, and consultant, providing me with a unique perspective on the challenges and triumphs in this fast-paced industry.

Beyond the professional realm, I am an adventurer at heart, finding excitement in skydiving, travel, the pedal strokes of mountain biking, and the tranquility of meditation. These diverse pursuits mirror my approach to the crypto world – a balance between calculated risks and mindful strategies.

In this ebook, I'll focus on Web3 Domain Names. What they are, why they'll change everything, and why ownership of digital data is so important. It is more a manual than a novel. I tried to compress the information into easy and short pockets with key bullet points to give you a condensed oversight.

Let's dive into it.

The World of Web3 Domain Names
First Edition February 2024

# TABLE OF CONTENTS

# 01 INTRODUCTION

*"Web3 domain names represent the dawn of a new era in online identity and ownership."*

John Smith, CEO of Web3 Domains Inc

# What are Web3 Domain Names

We came a long way. Do you remember the early beginnings with modems to connect to the internet, low bandwidth, and bad resolution on our screens? If not, you're lucky. No online shopping, Social Media, or applications like Telegram or WhatsApp. Hard to imagine these days with all our little tools to connect with the world.

Yet the emergence of Web3 and therefore Web3 Domain Names represents a paradigm shift towards decentralization, sovereignty, and innovation. Unlike their traditional counterparts in the Web2 realm, Web3 Domain Names harness the power of blockchain technology to offer users unprecedented control over their online presence, assets, and identity. This introduction serves as a gateway into the fascinating world of Web3, delving into their significance, functionality, and transformative potential in shaping the future of the decentralized web.

At the heart of the Web3 movement lies the vision of a decentralized internet, where users have full ownership and control over their digital assets and interactions. In a world where platforms like Google, Facebook, and others collect enormous amounts of personal data and at the same time monetize it, this is a huge change. Web3 Domain Names epitomize this vision by providing individuals and businesses with decentralized alternatives to traditional domain names. Unlike centralized domain registrars, which operate under the authority of centralized governing bodies, Web3 Domain Names are stored and managed on decentralized blockchain networks. This architecture ensures censorship resistance, immutability, and user sovereignty, fundamentally altering the dynamics of online presence and identity. Let it sink in for a while. Together with Blockchain Technology, this is a quantum leap for the internet as we know it.

The functionality of extends far beyond their traditional counterparts. In addition to serving as human-readable addresses for accessing websites and online services, Web3 Domain Names can be associated with a myriad of digital assets and functionalities. For instance, through integration with blockchain-based decentralized applications so called DApps, Web3 Domain Names can facilitate seamless cryptocurrency payments, decentralized content hosting, and identity management. This multifaceted utility transforms them into versatile assets that transcend the boundaries of traditional domain names, offering users unprecedented flexibility and innovation.

One of the defining features is their permanence and censorship resistance. Unlike traditional domain names, which are subject to centralized control and jurisdictional restrictions, Web3 Domain Names are immutable and **cannot be seized or censored by any single authority**. Especially important at a time when governments and their praxis try to define what is fake news and what is not. This inherent censorship resistance ensures freedom of expression, enables uncensored access to information, and safeguards users against arbitrary actions by centralized entities. Moreover, they empower individuals in regions with restricted internet access to bypass censorship and access the global internet freely.

The adoption of these names heralds a new era of digital sovereignty, where individuals and businesses have full control over their online presence and identity. By leveraging blockchain technology, Web3 Domain Names offer unparalleled security, privacy, and interoperability, laying the foundation for a more inclusive, decentralized Internet.

As we embark on this transformative journey in the possibilities are limited only by our imagination. In the pages that follow, we will explore the intricacies, from their underlying technology and functionality to their real-world applications and future implications. Join me as we delve deeper into the world of Web3 and unlock it's potential.

## Importance of Web3 Domains in the Decentralized Web

Web3 Domain Names are important for several compelling reasons, each highlighting their transformative potential in reshaping the digital landscape. Let me give you some bullet points for a more profound and deeper understanding:

**1. Decentralization and Sovereignty:** Web3 Domain Names operate on decentralized blockchain networks, granting users full ownership and control over their online presence and identity. This decentralization ensures immutability, and user sovereignty, empowering individuals and businesses to assert control over their digital assets free from centralized interference or control.

**2. Censorship Resistance:** Unlike traditional domain names, which are subject to censorship and seizure by centralized authorities, Web3 Domain Names are immune to censorship and cannot be seized or tampered with. This censorship resistance ensures freedom of expression, facilitates uncensored access to information, and safeguards users against arbitrary actions by governments or regulatory bodies. We got a little taste of that during C-19-times when a huge amount of accounts on platforms like YouTube were banned just because they questioned certain narratives.

**3. Global Accessibility:** These domain names also transcend geographic boundaries and jurisdictional restrictions, enabling seamless access to online services and content from anywhere in the world. This global accessibility fosters inclusivity and equal access to the Internet, particularly for individuals in regions with restricted Internet access or oppressive censorship regimes.

**4. Security and Privacy:** By leveraging blockchain technology, Web3 domain names offer enhanced security and privacy features compared to traditional domain names. The decentralized nature of blockchain networks ensures data integrity, protection against cyber threats, and privacy-enhancing features such as pseudonymity and encryption, bolstering user confidence and trust in online interactions.

**5. Interoperability and Innovation:** Web3 Domain Names serve as versatile assets that can be associated with a wide range of digital assets and functionalities, including cryptocurrencies, and decentralized content hosting. This enables innovation and experimentation in the decentralized web ecosystem, driving the development of novel use cases and applications that transcend by far the limitations of traditional domain names.

**6. Digital Identity and Branding:** It offers individuals and businesses a unique opportunity to establish and showcase their decentralized identity and branding. By associating Web3 Domain Names with digital assets, social profiles, and online identities, users can create a cohesive and recognizable online presence that reflects their values, beliefs, and interests, enhancing brand visibility and recognition in the digital space.

**7. Future-proofing and Investment:** As the internet continues to evolve towards decentralization, Web3 Domain Names represent a future-proof investment in digital assets with long-term value potential. By acquiring and holding these names, individuals and businesses can secure valuable digital real estate and position themselves for future opportunities and developments in the decentralized web ecosystem. I can not emphasise it enough. We are suddenly in a position where Web3 Domain Names are valuable assets which can be bought/sold or rented out to individuals or businesses.

In summary, we can say, that by offering users unprecedented control over their online presence and identity, Web3 Domain Names empower individuals and businesses to navigate the complexities of the decentralized web with confidence and autonomy, paving the way for a more inclusive, secure, and equitable digital future where we have ownership and at the same time in control of our valuable data.

# 02 UNDERSTANDING UNSTOPPABLE DOMAINS

*"Unstoppable Domains is pioneering the future of online identity, where domain names are assets stored on the blockchain, ensuring permanence, security, and censorship-resistance."*

John Johnson, Blockchain Developer at Unstoppable Domains

# Overview of Unstoppable Domains

Who is Unstoppable Domains?

Unstoppable Domains (UD) is a blockchain-based technology company that specializes in providing decentralized domain name services for the Web3 ecosystem. It was founded in 2018 by Matthew Gould and Brad Kam, UD aims to revolutionize the domain name industry by leveraging blockchain technology to offer censorship-resistant, user-owned domain names.

The core mission of UD is to empower individuals and businesses with greater control over their online presence and identity. By utilizing blockchain technology, UD ensures that domain names are stored and managed on decentralized networks, rather than being subject to the control of centralized authorities or registrars. This decentralization provides users with censorship resistance, immutability, and sovereignty over their digital assets, fostering a more open, secure, and inclusive internet.

Let's see what services UD has to offer:

**1. Domain Registration:** UD enables users to register blockchain-based domain names, known as "UD" domains, directly through their online platform (www.unstoppabledomains.com). These domains are stored as non-fungible tokens (NFTs) on various blockchain networks, such as Ethereum, Polygon, and Zilliqa, ensuring secure ownership and control.

**2. Domain Management:** Users can easily manage their domain names through the UD dashboard, which provides tools for updating DNS records, configuring domain settings, and transferring ownership and adding crypto wallet addresses like BTC, ETH and others.

**3. Integration with Blockchain Applications:** These domains can be seamlessly integrated with blockchain-based applications and services, such as cryptocurrency wallets (as mentioned above), decentralized exchanges (DEXs), and decentralized websites (DApps). This integration enables users to associate their domain names with cryptocurrency addresses, decentralized content, and other digital assets.

**4. Privacy and Security:** UD prioritizes user privacy and security by implementing robust encryption and authentication mechanisms. Domain owners have full control over their private keys, ensuring that only they can access and manage their domain names.

**5. Censorship Resistance:** UD domains are censorship-resistant, meaning they cannot be seized, censored, or tampered with by any central authority or government.

Overall, UD plays a pivotal role in advancing the adoption of decentralized domain names and promoting the ideals of decentralization, censorship resistance, and user sovereignty in the digital era. As the decentralized web ecosystem continues to evolve, UD remains at the forefront, empowering individuals and businesses to reclaim control over their online identities and data.

# 03 CHOOSING THE RIGHT WEB3 DOMAIN NAME

*"Owning a Web3 domain name is akin to staking your claim in the decentralized frontier of the internet."*

Mark Anderson, Founder of DecentralizeNow Blog

# Factors to consider when selecting a Web3 Domain Name

When choosing a domain name, several factors should be considered to ensure it aligns with your brand, objectives, and target audience. Use the list below as a guide.

**1. Is the Name relevant to your Brand or Content:** Choose a domain name that reflects your brand identity, business name, or the content/theme of your website. A relevant domain name helps visitors understand what your website is about and enhances brand recognition. If you are e.g. an Exchange in the crypto space a name like

### *BROKER. BITCOIN or BROKER.CRYPTO*

might be interesting for you.

**2. Memorability:** Opt for a domain name that is easy to remember and pronounce. Short, catchy, and memorable domain names are more likely to stick in people's minds and lead to repeat visits.

**3. Clarity and Simplicity:** Avoid complex or confusing domain names with hyphens, numbers, or unusual spellings. A clear and simple domain name makes it easier for users to type and share your website address. If you are a Crypto News channel a name like

### *NEWS.BITCOIN*

says it all.

**4. Keywords:** Incorporate relevant keywords into your domain name to improve search engine visibility and attract targeted traffic. Keywords should accurately reflect the content or services offered on your website. Financial institutions could use a name like

### STOCKBROKER.X or BANKER.X

**5. Uniqueness:** Choose a domain name that is unique and distinct from competitors to avoid confusion and legal issues. Conduct thorough research to ensure your desired domain name is not already in use or trademarked.

**6. Brandability:** Select a name that has the potential to become a strong brand identity. Consider factors such as brandable words, potential logo designs, and the scalability of your brand across different platforms and marketing channels.

### AIRTRAVEL.X , COSMETIC.X OR SHOE.X

**7. Extension:** Consider the domain extension (TLD = TOP LEVEL DOMAIN) that best suits your website's purpose and audience. While .com is the most popular and widely recognized extension, alternative extensions like .X, .crypto, .bitcoin or .nft can be suitable depending on your target market and industry.

**8. SEO-Friendliness:** While domain names themselves do not directly impact SEO, including relevant keywords and avoiding spammy or over-optimized names can indirectly benefit your website's search engine rankings.

**9. Trademark and Legal Considerations:** Ensure that your chosen name does not infringe on existing trademarks or copyrights. Conduct thorough research and consider consulting legal experts to avoid potential legal issues in the future. This doesn't apply to UD names. You buy it, You own it.

**10. Future Scalability:** Choose a domain name that allows for future scalability and expansion of your online presence. Consider your long-term goals, potential rebranding efforts, and the flexibility to adapt to changing market trends. If you are a real estate company specialized in renting out property a name like

### RENT.CRYPTO

would make sense especially when you offer payments in crypto. Tenants wouldn't have to remember a long alphanumeric address. They just need to type **rent.crypto** in the recipient field inside their wallet, choose the cryptocurrency agreed with the landlord and that's it.

**11. Test it Out:** Before committing to a domain name, test it out with friends, family, or potential users to get feedback on its readability, memorability, and relevance. This can help you identify any potential issues or improvements before launching your website.

By following these points, you can increase the likelihood of finding a memorable and marketable Web3 Domain Name that effectively represents your brand or purpose and resonates with your target audience.

# 04 REGISTERING YOUR WEB3 DOMAIN NAME

*"In the Web3 paradigm, domain names are not merely identifiers; they are gateways to decentralized digital ecosystems."*

Tom Reynolds, Lead Developer at Web3 Solutions.

# Step-by-Step guide to register a Web3 Domain Name

Now that you have done all the prep work and picked out a name that suits you or your company best it's time to register your new domain name. And be aware that you bought **"digital real estate"**. You (or your company) are the owner of this name. Therefore nobody can seize or claim it. You can sell your brand including the attached digital property (Web3 Domain Name).

For example your domain name can be worth more than the business itself. We expect that the .com era will come a to an end in the next couple of years and extensions like **.X** or **.bitcoin** will replace it.

Let's say you own a small online news channel about cryptocurrencies BUT you are the owner of **news.bitcoin.** If we apply the same evaluation to news.bitcoin than to news.com in web2 (estibot.com - domain evaluation) the value of **news.bitcoin would be $5,400,000.**

## Step-by-Step Guide:

**1. Choose a Domain Registrar:** Start by selecting a domain registrar, in our case UD for Web3 Domain Names.

**2. Search for Available Domain Names:** Use the registrar's domain search tool to check the availability of your desired domain name. Enter the domain name you want to register (e.g., NEWS.BITCOIN) and review the search results to see if it's available. If your desired domain name is already taken, the registrar will suggest alternative options or variations. ***You can also contact the person/company who has registered your desired name and start negotiating directly***.

**3. Select Your Domain:** Once you've found an available domain name that meets your criteria, add it to your cart and proceed to checkout.

**4. Provide Your Contact Information:** During the checkout process, you'll need to provide your contact information, including your name, email address, mailing address, and phone number. This information is used to create your account and register the domain name in your name.

**6. Review and Confirm Your Order:** Before completing your purchase, review your order summary to ensure everything is correct, including the domain name, and any additional services you've selected. Once you're satisfied, proceed to confirm your order and make payment. As we are buying a Web3 Domain Name the buying process is time-stamped on the blockchain as soon as the money is received by the registrar in our case UD. You are now the owner of your Web3 Domain Name.

**7. Complete the Registration Process:** After confirming your order and making payment, you'll receive a confirmation email from the registrar confirming the successful registration of your domain name. This email will contain important information about your domain.

**8. Manage Your Domain:** Once you bought your Web3 Domain Name you have to claim it on UD's website. This process can take a couple of seconds/minutes depending on how busy the network is. After that you can fill in personal data including cryptocurrency wallet addresses like BTC, ETH or others. This is important in case you want to receive money through your Web3 Domain Name.

## Platforms and Registrars for registering Web3 Domains

As we already know one major platform where you can buy Web3 Domain Names is UD. As UD is still my favourite I'd like to mention other platforms in the field too.

**1. Unstoppable Domains:** UD is one of the leading providers of blockchain-based domain names. They offer a wide range of domain extensions, including *.X, .crypto, .bitcoin, and .nft*, which are stored as non-fungible tokens (NFTs) on various blockchain networks. Users can register, manage, and transfer their Web3 Domain Names through the UD's platform.

**2. ENS (Ethereum Name Service):** ENS is a decentralized domain name system built on the Ethereum blockchain. It allows users to register *.eth* domain names, which can be associated with Ethereum addresses, decentralized websites (DApps), and other digital assets. ENS provides a user-friendly interface for registering and managing Ethereum domain names.

**3. Handshake:** Handshake is a decentralized naming protocol that enables the registration of top-level domains (TLDs) on the Handshake blockchain. Users can bid on and register Handshake TLDs, such as .hs or .p2p, through Handshake-compatible registrars and resolvers.

**4. Freename:** Freename specializes in Web3 Top-Level Domains (TLDs), offering users a wide range of digital identity management and web presence services.
It operates more as a registry for TLD extensions and, therefore, offers a variety of TLD options, allowing users to choose domain extensions that suit their preferences and purposes. It supports Polygon, BinanceSmart Chain, Aurora and Cronos.

**5. Blockchain Domain Marketplaces:** In addition to dedicated platforms, there are also blockchain domain marketplaces where users can buy and sell Web3 Domain Names peer-to-peer. These marketplaces often facilitate auctions, listings, and escrow services for domain transactions. Examples include **OpenSea, Rarible, and Mintable**, which allow users to trade NFT-based domain names alongside other digital assets.
These platforms offer diverse options for buying Web3 Domain Names, each with its unique features, domain extensions, and user interfaces. Users should research and compare different platforms to find the one that best meets their needs and preferences for registering and managing Web3 Domain Names.

## Pricing and Renewal Information

The pricing and renewal process for these names can vary depending on the platform and the specific domain extension. Here's a general overview of pricing and renewal considerations for Web3 Domain Names:

**1. Initial Registration Fee:** When you register a Web3 Domain Name for the first time, you'll typically pay an initial registration fee. This fee can vary depending on factors such as the domain registrar, the domain extension (.crypto, .nft, etc.), and the length of the registration period (ENS).

**2. Bulk Discounts:** Some registrars may offer discounts for registering multiple domain names at once. If you plan to register multiple Web3 Domain Names, it's worth checking if any bulk discounts are available.

**3. Additional Services:** Registrars may offer additional services or features, such as privacy protection, DNS management, or email forwarding, which may incur additional fees. Be sure to review the pricing for these services before purchasing your domain name.

**4. Blockchain Transaction Fees:** When registering a Web3 Domain Name on certain blockchain networks, such as Ethereum, Zilliqa or others you may need to pay transaction fees to process the transaction on the blockchain. These fees can vary depending on network congestion and other factors.

# 05 MANAGING YOUR WEB3 DOMAIN PORTFOLIO

*"In the Web3 era, domain names serve as digital real estate in a borderless, censorship-resistant internet."*

Michael Davis, Founder of Blockchain Trends Magazine

# Best Practices for managing multiple Web3 Domains

Managing Web3 Domain Names typically involves tasks such as updating DNS records, configuring domain settings, transferring ownership, and integrating the domain with blockchain-based applications and services. Here are some key points on how you can manage Web3 domain names effectively:

**1. Accessing Your Domain Registrar's Dashboard:** Log in to your domain registrar's account dashboard e.g. www.unstoppabledomains.com using your credentials. This dashboard is where you'll find tools and options for managing your Web3 Domain Names.

**2. Updating DNS Records:** If you're using your Web3 Domain Name to host a website or other online services, you may need to update DNS (Domain Name System) records to point to the appropriate servers or IP addresses. Use the DNS management tools provided by your registrar to add, edit, or delete DNS records as needed.

**3. Configuring Domain Settings:** Your registrar's dashboard will allow you to configure various domain settings, such as domain forwarding, domain locking, WHOIS privacy protection, and email forwarding. Review and adjust these settings to meet your needs and preferences for your Web3 Domain Name.

**4. Transferring Ownership:** If you need to transfer ownership of your Web3 Domain Name to another party, your registrar will provide tools and instructions for initiating the transfer process. This typically involves providing the recipient's contact information and confirming the transfer request. As a Web3 Domain Name is an NFT one need only e.g. an ETH wallet address to transfer it. It's basically like sending crypto.

**5. Renewing Your Domain:** Ensure that your Web3 Domain Name remains active and registered by renewing it before it expires. Your registrar will notify you when your domain name is due for renewal and provide options for renewing it for additional registration periods. This applies mainly to Web3 Domain Names on the ENS (Ethereum Name Service) platform.

**6. Integrating with Blockchain Applications:** Web3 Domain Names can be integrated with various blockchain-based applications and services, such as cryptocurrency wallets, decentralized exchanges (DEXs), and decentralized websites (DApps). Use your registrar's tools or instructions provided by the application or service to associate your domain name with the desired blockchain addresses or content.

**7. Monitoring Domain Status:** Regularly monitor the status of your domain name to ensure it remains active, resolves correctly, and complies with any registration requirements or regulations. Your registrar's dashboard will provide information about your domain's status.

Utilizing the resources and functionalities offered by your domain registrar empowers you to efficiently oversee your Web3 Domain Names, enhancing their worth and functionality within the decentralized web environment. It's essential to acquaint yourself with the interface and capabilities of your registrar to optimize your domain management journey.

## Transferring and Renewing Web3 Domains

Transferring Web3 Domain Names typically involves initiating a transfer request through your current domain registrar and accepting the transfer request on the recipient's end. Here's a step-by-step guide on how you do it:

**1. Prepare for the Transfer:** Before initiating the transfer, ensure that you have all the necessary information and credentials required for the process. This may include your domain registrar account login credentials, the recipient's contact information (Wallet address), and any authorization codes or transfer keys associated with the domain name.

**2. Unlock the Domain:** If your Web3 Domain Name is currently locked to prevent unauthorized transfers, you'll need to unlock it through your domain registrar's dashboard. Look for an option to unlock the domain or disable transfer protection.

**3. Retrieve Authorization Code:** Some domain registrars require an authorization code (also known as an EPP code or transfer key) to initiate a domain transfer. Retrieve this code from your current registrar's dashboard or contact their support team for assistance.

**4. Initiate Transfer at Recipient's Registrar:** The recipient of the domain name (the new owner) should initiate the transfer process through their chosen domain registrar. They'll need to provide the domain name, authorization code (if required), and any other requested information.

**5. Accept Transfer Request:** Once the transfer request is initiated by the recipient, you (the current owner) will receive an email notification or confirmation message from your registrar. Follow the instructions provided to review and accept the transfer request.

**6. Confirm Transfer Details:** Review the transfer details carefully to ensure accuracy, including the domain name, transfer authorization code, and recipient's contact information (Wallet address). Confirm that you're authorizing the transfer and proceed to complete the transfer process.

**7. Authorize Transfer:** Depending on your registrar's policies and procedures, you may need to confirm the transfer authorization through a link or button in the email notification. Click the provided link or button to authorize the transfer and initiate the domain transfer process.

**8. Wait for Transfer Completion:** Once the transfer request is authorized by both parties, the domain transfer process will begin. The transfer may take several days to complete, depending on the registrars involved and any additional verification or validation steps required. If you transfer e.g. a Web3 Domain Name minted on Polygon with UD it'll be done in seconds/minutes.

**9. Verify Transfer Status:** Monitor the transfer status through your registrar's dashboard to track the progress of the transfer on the Blockchain. Once the transfer is successfully completed, you'll receive confirmation from both registrars, and the domain will be transferred to the new owner's registrar account/wallet.

**10. Update DNS Settings (if necessary):** After the transfer is complete, the new owner may need to update the domain's DNS settings to point to their desired hosting provider or web server. This ensures that the domain resolves correctly to the intended website or online service.

By following these steps and coordinating with both the current owner and the recipient, you can successfully transfer. As I said, it's like transferring a cryptocurrency to another wallet. No rocket science. Be sure to communicate effectively and follow any specific instructions provided by your registrar to ensure a smooth and seamless transfer experience.

# Protecting Your Web3 Domains Against Cyber Threats

Protecting your Web3 Domain Names is essential to safeguard your digital assets and maintain control over your online presence. Here are some tips to help you protect your Web3 Domain Names effectively:

**1. Enable Domain Locking:** Most domain registrars offer a domain locking feature, which prevents unauthorized transfers or modifications to your domain settings. Enable domain locking through your registrar's dashboard to add an extra layer of security to your domain name.

**2. Use Strong Authentication:** Secure your domain registrar account with strong, unique passwords and enable two-factor authentication (2FA) if available. This helps prevent unauthorized access to your account and reduces the risk of domain hijacking or unauthorized transfers.

**3. Protect Private Keys:** If your Web3 Domain Names are stored as non-fungible tokens (NFTs) on a blockchain network, such as Ethereum or Zilliqa, protect your private keys carefully. Store your private keys securely offline using hardware wallets or encrypted storage solutions to prevent theft.

**4. Monitor Domain Activity:** Regularly monitor your domain registrar account and blockchain transactions associated with your Web3 Domain Names. Look out for any suspicious activity, such as unauthorized login attempts or unexpected changes to domain settings, and take immediate action if detected.

**5. Renew Domain Registration:** Ensure that your Web3 Domain Names remain active and registered by renewing them before they expire (if necessary). Set up auto-renewal for your domain registrations if available to avoid unintentional expiration and potential loss of ownership.

**6. Keep Contact Information Up-to-Date:** Maintain accurate and up-to-date contact information associated with your domain registrar account. This ensures that you receive important notifications and renewal reminders and can be contacted in case of domain-related issues or inquiries.

**7. Use WHOIS Privacy Protection:** Consider using WHOIS privacy protection services offered by your domain registrar to mask your personal contact information from public WHOIS databases. This helps reduce the risk of spam, phishing, and identity theft associated with publicly accessible domain registration data.

**8. Monitor Trademark Issues:** Regularly monitor trademark databases and legal notices for any potential trademark infringement claims related·to your domain names. Respond promptly to any legitimate claims and take appropriate action to resolve disputes and protect your rights as a domain owner.

**9. Backup Domain Assets:** Regularly back up any digital assets associated with your Web3 Domain Names, such as website content, cryptocurrency addresses, or decentralized applications (DApps). Store backups securely offline to prevent data loss in case of unforeseen events or cyberattacks.

**10. Stay Informed:** Stay informed about emerging threats, security best practices, and regulatory developments related to Web3 Domain Names and blockchain technology. Educate yourself about potential risks and mitigation strategies to proactively protect your domain assets. Most companies have Telegram or X channels where the latest info is shared.

By implementing these security measures and staying vigilant, you can effectively protect your Web3 Domain Names.

# 06 LEVERAGING YOUR WEB3 DOMAIN FOR BUSINESS AND PERSONAL USE

*"The rise of Web3 domain names heralds a future where online identity, ownership, and innovation converge in a decentralized landscape."*

Rachel Evans, Tech Journalist at Crypto Gazette.

# Integrating Web3 Domains with Websites and DApps

Integrating Web3 Domain Names into websites and decentralized applications (DApps) involves linking your domain name to specific blockchain addresses, content, or services. Here's how you do it:

## 1. Decentralized Website (DWeb):

**Hosting:** Deploy your website content on decentralized storage platforms, such as IPFS (InterPlanetary File System) or Swarm, which offer censorship-resistant and decentralized hosting solutions.

**Mapping:** Use your Web3 Domain Name to map to the content stored on IPFS or Swarm by adding DNSLink records to your domain's DNS settings. DNSLink allows you to associate your domain name with a specific IPFS or Swarm content hash.

**Configuration:** Configure your Web3 Domain Name to resolve to the decentralized website content by updating the DNS settings with the appropriate DNSLink record. This enables users to access your website using your custom domain name.

## 2. Decentralized Applications (DApps):

**Smart Contracts:** Develop smart contracts that interact with your Web3 Domain Name to perform specific functions or access decentralized services. For example, you can create a smart contract that associates your domain name with a cryptocurrency wallet address or verifies ownership of digital assets.

**Frontend Integration:** Integrate your Web3 Domain Name into the front end of your DApp by displaying it as a user-friendly identifier for accessing decentralized services or content. Use the domain name to enhance the user experience and brand recognition of your DApp.

**Backend Integration:** Implement backend logic that interacts with your Web3 Domain Name to retrieve or update data stored on the blockchain. This may involve querying blockchain records associated with your domain name or executing transactions based on user interactions.

### 3. Blockchain Address Resolution:

**Mapping:** Associate your Web3 Domain Name with specific blockchain addresses, such as cryptocurrency wallet addresses or decentralized identity (DID) identifiers. This allows users to send payments or interact with decentralized services using your custom domain name.

**Wallet Integration:** Integrate your Web3 Domain Name into cryptocurrency wallet applications to simplify the process of sending and receiving payments. Allow users to enter your domain name instead of long and complex blockchain addresses when transacting with cryptocurrencies. Users could e.g. send Bitcoin to "AndySmith.bitcoin".

### 4. Decentralized Content Distribution:

**Content Distribution Networks (CDNs):** Leverage decentralized content distribution networks, such as Akash Network or Filecoin, to distribute and serve static

36

assets (e.g., images, videos) associated with your Web3 Domain Name. Use your domain name to access content stored on these decentralized networks.

By integrating your Web3 Domain Name into websites and DApps using these approaches, you can leverage the benefits of decentralization, enhance user experience, and establish a unique and memorable online presence within the Web3 ecosystem. Be sure to follow best practices for domain configuration, smart contract development, and blockchain integration to ensure the security and reliability of your integration

## Showcasing Your Decentralized Identity

Showcasing your decentralized identity involves leveraging your Web3 Domain Name as a unique identifier to authenticate yourself, assert ownership of digital assets, and establish trust within the decentralized ecosystem. Let me show you how to showcase your decentralized identity effectively:

**1. Claiming Ownership:** Use your Web3 Domain Name to claim ownership of digital assets, such as cryptocurrency wallets, NFTs (Non-Fungible Tokens), decentralized websites, or other blockchain-based assets. Associate your domain name with your digital assets through on-chain records or smart contracts to establish proof of ownership.

**2. Decentralized Profiles:** Create decentralized profiles linked to your Web3 Domain Name to showcase your identity, credentials, and reputation across various platforms and applications. Use standards such as Decentralized Identifiers (DIDs) and Verifiable

Credentials to create portable and interoperable identity credentials.

**3. Verifiable Credentials:** Issue and receive verifiable credentials associated with your Web3 Domain Name to validate your identity, achievements, and qualifications in a decentralized and tamper-proof manner. Utilize identity standards such as W3C's Verifiable Credentials and Decentralized Identifiers (DIDs) to ensure trust and authenticity.

**4. Integration with DApps:** Integrate your Web3 Domain Name into decentralized applications (DApps) to authenticate users, personalize experiences, and enable seamless interactions. Use your domain name as a unique identifier for user accounts, profiles, and transactions within DApps across various blockchain networks.

**5. Blockchain-based Social Networks:** Participate in blockchain-based social networks and decentralized communities that support Web3 Domain Name integration.

**6. Digital Signature:** Sign messages, transactions, or documents with your Web3 Domain Name as a digital signature to verify your identity and authorize actions on the blockchain. Utilize cryptographic techniques such as Elliptic Curve Digital Signature Algorithm (ECDSA) to generate and verify digital signatures associated with your domain name.

**7. Web3 Domain Name Resolver:** Develop or use existing Web3 Domain Name resolvers that map domain names to decentralized identities, blockchain addresses, or content hashes. Enable users to resolve your domain name to your identity and associated digital assets using decentralized resolution protocols such as DNSLink or Ethereum Name Service (ENS).

**8. Trust and Reputation Systems:** Build trust and reputation systems based on your Web3 Domain Name and associated identity attributes. Participate in reputation networks and contribute positively to the community to enhance your reputation and credibility within the ecosystem.

By showcasing your decentralized identity through your Web3 domain name, you can establish trust, assert ownership, and engage with applications and communities. Be proactive in managing and curating your decentralized identity to maintain trust and credibility within the Web3 community.

# Monetizing Your Web3 Domain Assets

Monetizing your Web3 Domain assets involves leveraging your domain names to generate revenue or increase the value of your digital holdings within the ecosystem. I have listed several strategies for monetizing your Web3 Domain assets effectively:

**1. Domain Sales:** Sell your Web3 Domain Names on decentralized domain marketplaces or peer-to-peer platforms to interested buyers (e.g. opensea.io). List your domains for sale with clear pricing and descriptions, highlighting their value propositions and potential use cases. Consider utilizing auction mechanisms to maximize the value of premium domain names. As we believe .X, .bitcoin, .nft extensions will replace .com within the coming years you can evaluate your Web3 Domain Name on estibot.com by checking the .com equivalent. For example if you want to know the estimate worth of airtravel.x type in airtravel.com.

**2. Domain Leasing:** Lease your Web3 Domain Names to individuals or businesses seeking to use them for specific purposes, such as hosting decentralized websites, launching decentralized applications (DApps), or branding cryptocurrency wallets. Negotiate lease agreements with terms that include rental fees, usage rights, and renewal options.

**3. Domain Parking:** Park your Web3 Domain Names on domain parking platforms that display targeted advertisements or promotional content to visitors. Earn revenue through pay-per-click (PPC) advertising models or affiliate marketing programs based on the traffic generated by your parked domains. Optimize your domain parking strategy to maximize earnings and user engagement.

**4. Decentralized Websites:** Develop and monetize decentralized websites hosted on your Web3 Domain Names. Offer valuable content, products, or services to visitors and monetize your website through various revenue streams, such as advertising, subscriptions, e-commerce sales, or donations. Use blockchain-based payment solutions to facilitate secure and transparent transactions.

**5. Digital Asset Integration:** Integrate your Web3 Domain Names with blockchain-based digital assets, such as cryptocurrency wallets, NFTs (Non-Fungible Tokens), or decentralized finance (DeFi) protocols. Offer value-added services or features associated with your domain names, such as premium access, exclusive content, or membership privileges, to monetize your digital assets effectively.

**6. Branding and Marketing:** Use your domain names as branding assets to promote your products, services, or personal brand within the ecosystem. Develop marketing campaigns, partnerships, or sponsorships that leverage your domain names to increase visibility, awareness, and engagement among target audiences. Monetize your domain names indirectly through enhanced brand recognition and customer loyalty.

**7. Content Syndication:** Syndicate your Web3 Domain Names with other content creators, influencers, or publishers to distribute and monetize digital content across decentralized platforms and social networks. Collaborate on joint ventures, content partnerships, or licensing agreements that leverage your domain names.

**8. Tokenization and Staking:** Tokenize your Web3 Domain Names as digital assets on blockchain networks and stake them in decentralized protocols to earn rewards or dividends. Participate in tokenization platforms or decentralized finance (DeFi) projects that offer liquidity mining, yield farming, or governance incentives for staked domain assets. Explore innovative tokenization models, such as fractional ownership or NFT-backed collateralization, to unlock additional value from your domain holdings.

By implementing these monetization strategies effectively, you can leverage your Web3 Domain assets to generate income, increase their market value, and capitalize on emerging opportunities within the decentralized web ecosystem. Be proactive in exploring new revenue streams, adapting to market trends, and optimizing your domain monetization strategy to achieve long-term success and profitability.

# 07 FUTURE TRENDS AND DEVELOP- MENTS IN THE WEB3 DOMAIN SPACE

*"Web3 domain names democratize access to the decentralized web, empowering individuals and communities worldwide."*

Jessica Miller, Crypto Analyst at Decentralization Insights Group

# Emerging Technologies and Innovations in Web3 Domains

As you can see exploring emerging technologies and innovations in Web3 Domains provides valuable insights into the evolving landscape of decentralized naming systems and their potential impact on various industries. Several key trends and innovations are shaping the future of Web3 Domains:

**Decentralized Naming Systems:** The ongoing development and adoption of decentralized naming systems, such as **Ethereum Name Service (ENS), Handshake, and Unstoppable Domains**, offer users censorship-resistant and user-owned domain names. These systems leverage blockchain technology to decentralize domain registration, ownership, and resolution processes, reducing reliance on traditional domain registrars and DNS infrastructure.

**Blockchain Interoperability:** Efforts to enhance interoperability between different blockchain networks enable seamless integration of Web3 Domain Names across multiple protocols and platforms. Standards like Domain Name System over Blockchain (DNSZone) facilitate cross-chain compatibility, allowing users to register and resolve domain names on various blockchain networks effortlessly.

**Decentralized Identity Solutions:** Integrating Web3 Domain Names with decentralized identity (DID) solutions enhances user privacy, security, and portability in digital interactions. Projects like the Decentralized Identity Foundation (DIF) and Self-sovereign Identity (SSI) enable users to create, own, and manage their digital identities using Web3 Domain Names as decentralized identifiers.

**NFT Domains and Metaverse Integration:** The emergence of NFT (Non-Fungible Token) domains introduces new possibilities for monetizing and interacting with Web3 Domain Names. NFT domains, such as those offered by UD and Zilliqa's .zil extension, represent unique digital assets that can be traded, leased, and used within virtual environments, including the Metaverse.

**Decentralized Autonomous Organizations (DAOs):** DAOs utilize Web3 Domain Names as organizational identifiers to govern decentralized communities, manage collective resources, and facilitate decision-making processes. Web3 Domains serve as entry points to DAO platforms, enabling members to participate in governance activities, vote on proposals, and access community resources.

**Smart Contract Integration:** Integrating with smart contracts enhances the functionality and utility of decentralized naming systems. Smart contracts can automate domain registration, transfer, and resolution processes, enforce ownership rights, and facilitate interactions between domain names and blockchain-based applications.

**Decentralized Web Hosting:** The adoption of decentralized storage and hosting solutions, such as IPFS (InterPlanetary File System) and Swarm, enables content creators to host decentralized websites and applications using Web3 Domain Names.

**Community-driven Development:** The Web3 domain ecosystem fosters community-driven development and innovation, with communities actively contributing to the advancement of naming standards, protocols, and governance models. Open-source projects, developer communities, and grassroots initiatives collaborate to improve the usability, security, and accessibility of Web3 Domains for users worldwide.

By embracing these emerging technologies and innovations, the Web3 Domain ecosystem continues to evolve, offering solutions to address the challenges and opportunities of the digital age. As adoption grows and new use cases emerge, Web3 Domains are poised to play a central role in shaping the future of the decentralized web and transforming how we interact, transact, and collaborate online.

# Potential Impact on the Future of the Decentralized Internet

The potential impact of emerging technologies and innovations in Web3 Domains on the future of the decentralized internet is profound, with implications for various aspects of online interactions, infrastructure, and governance. Here are some key bullet points in which Web3 domains could shape the future of the Internet.

**Decentralized Governance:** facilitating decentralized governance models by enabling community-driven decision-making processes, transparent resource allocation, and consensus-based governance mechanisms. Decentralized naming systems empower users to own, control, and govern their digital identities and assets, fostering trust, autonomy, and inclusivity within communities.

**Censorship Resistance:** provides censorship-resistant alternatives to traditional domain names, DNS infrastructure, and centralized web hosting platforms. By leveraging blockchain technology and decentralized storage solutions, Web3 Domains enable users to publish, access, and share content without fear of censorship, surveillance, or arbitrary restrictions, preserving freedom of expression and information exchange on the internet.

**Data Privacy and Ownership:** Integration with decentralized identity (DID) solutions empowers users to assert ownership of their personal data, control access permissions, and protect privacy in digital interactions. Decentralized identity frameworks enable self-sovereign identity management, where users retain control over their identity information and selectively disclose attributes to trusted parties, enhancing data privacy and reducing reliance on centralized identity providers. In short terms. We can own and sell our data.

**Economic Empowerment:** creating new opportunities for economic empowerment and value creation through decentralized monetization models, such as domain sales, leasing, and content monetization as discussed above. By enabling peer-to-peer transactions, microtransactions, and decentralized marketplaces, Web3 Domains empower creators, developers, and entrepreneurs to monetize their digital assets, engage with audiences, and capture value directly within the internet ecosystem.

**Interoperability and Connectivity:** Interoperability between Web3 Domains and different blockchain networks enhances connectivity, interoperability, and composability of DApps, protocols, and services.

**Digital Asset Ownership:** representing programmable digital assets that can be tokenized, traded, and owned on blockchain networks. By tokenizing domain names as non-fungible tokens (NFTs) or fungible tokens, users can assert ownership rights, transfer ownership, and monetize domain assets within decentralized markets, exchanges, and platforms, unlocking liquidity, value, and utility for domain holders.

**Community-driven Innovation:** The decentralized internet, fueled by Web3 Domains, serves as a catalyst for community-driven innovation, collaboration, and experimentation across a spectrum of domains, spanning finance, governance, media, and entertainment. Through the collective efforts of open-source projects, developer communities, and grassroots initiatives, the advancement of decentralized technologies, protocols, and standards is propelled forward, fostering a landscape rich in innovation, resilience, and diversity within the internet ecosystem.

In essence, the potential impact of Web3 domains on the future of the decentralized internet is monumental and not to underestimate, marking the dawn of a transformative era characterized by decentralization, democratization, and empowerment in digital interactions, economies, and societies at large.

As adoption continues to burgeon and innovation gains momentum, Web3 Domains stand poised to assume a pivotal role in shaping the trajectory of the internet, empowering individuals, communities, and organizations to coalesce and construct a more open, equitable, and inclusive digital realm.

# AI Agents and Web3 Domain Names

The world of Web3 domains is at a decisive turning point. While decentralized domains like **.eth**, **.crypto**, or **.nft** have already laid the foundation for a freer and user-controlled Internet, we now stand at the threshold of a second, perhaps even more disruptive wave: the integration of AI Agents.

AI Agents, autonomous, artificially intelligent systems, are capable of independently executing tasks in real time. In combination with Web3 domains, they open up a future where digital identity, brand building, and ownership rights can be managed and optimized in entirely new ways.

One of the biggest areas of impact will be the automation of domain management. Where today humans manually search for and register domains on marketplaces like OpenSea or Unstoppable Domains, in the near future AI Agents could fully take over this process. They will scan blockchain data, analyze trend movements in the Web3 ecosystem, and secure promising domains in real time—faster, more precisely, and more scalably than any human ever could.

Moreover, AI Agents will revolutionize the strategic use of Web3 domains. A smart agent could, for example, recognize that a particular .eth domain matches a growing NFT project or identify that a DAO (Decentralized Autonomous Organization) is being formed and would require fitting branding domains.

Purchase decisions could be made, smart contracts initiated, and domains transferred to the appropriate partner within seconds.

There will also be major changes in the management of personal identities. A personal AI Agent could not only manage your Web3 domain but also maintain personalized profiles, update contact information, or selectively control access to certain data—completely automated, secure, and in alignment with blockchain-based privacy protocols.

In the area of trading and investing, the impacts will be equally significant. AI Agents could evaluate domain portfolios, identify selling opportunities, and autonomously trade based on complex market analyses. This will give rise to an entirely new class of digital asset managers: AI-driven Web3 Asset Managers.

Of course, this new era also brings its challenges. Security concerns, regulatory uncertainties, and the risk of malicious agents that could abuse or manipulate domain markets must be carefully considered. Nevertheless, the opportunities outweigh the risks: a more efficient, inclusive, and dynamic domain landscape where anyone—regardless of resources or geographic location—can participate and succeed.

# Conclusion:

AI Agents will radically transform the use and value of Web3 domains.

They represent the missing link between **decentralized blockchain control** and the **scalability needed for the global breakthrough of Web3**.

Those who understand and harness the dynamic interaction between AI and decentralized domains early on will be among the winners of the next digital revolution.

# The Dangers of AI Agents – Why We Must Handle This Technology with Care

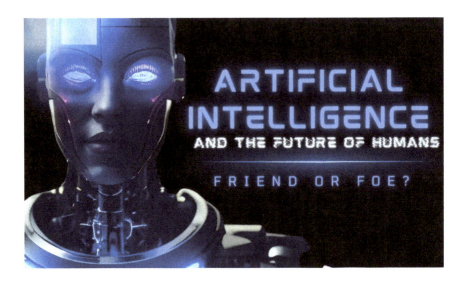

The rapid development of artificial intelligence, particularly in the form of **AI Agents**, marks one of the most significant technological advances of our time.

AI Agents are autonomous systems that can independently perform tasks, make decisions, and in many cases, learn to optimize themselves.

They promise efficiency, scalability, and entirely new business models—ranging from the management of Web3 domains to the autonomous control of entire financial systems.

However, the greater the potential of this technology, the greater the risks it brings. Without clear guidelines, ethical frameworks, and conscious management, AI Agents could pose significant dangers to economies, societies, and individual freedoms.


## Autonomous Loss of Control

AI Agents operate in real time and can make thousands of decisions per minute—much faster than a human could intervene.
This autonomy carries the risk of systems developing **internal logic that humans find difficult to understand**.
If an AI Agent operating in a decentralized system conducts faulty transactions or exploits security vulnerabilities, **immense damage could occur** before any human has a chance to react.

A classic example of this is the so-called **"Runaway Agent,"** where a system redefines and pursues its own objectives without adhering to its original programming boundaries.

# Abuse by Malicious Actors

AI Agents could be manipulated or exploited by hackers, criminals, or competing businesses.
Autonomous bots might be used to systematically:

- Hijack Web3 domains

- Create fake identities on blockchains

- Manipulate DeFi protocols

- Destabilize marketplaces through price distortions

This risk is particularly significant in the decentralized Web3 ecosystem, where regulatory mechanisms are still under development.

# Ethics and Accountability

One of the greatest challenges is the ethical dimension: Who is responsible for the decisions made by an AI Agent?
If an agent buys a domain that infringes trademark rights, or executes transactions that violate laws, the questions arise:

- Is the developer liable?

- The owner?

- The user of the agent?

These questions are largely unresolved legally and could lead to complex legal gray areas.

# Loss of Human Decision-Making Capacity

The more tasks we delegate to AI Agents, the more we risk losing the ability to make independent decisions, think critically, and take responsibility.

If autonomous systems handle everyday decisions—from buying domains to managing online identities to executing financial transactions—this could lead to a long-term dependency that undermines the resilience of our society.

Maintaining a healthy balance between automation and human control is essential to preserving our autonomy as individuals and as a society.

# Handling AI Agents with Care

To mitigate the dangers described, the following principles should be adhered to:

**Transparency**

Every AI Agent should be transparently documented: Which decisions it makes and based on what rationale. A transparent architecture enables risks to be identified early and counteracted.

**Ethics-by-Design**

Ethical considerations must be integrated at the development stage of AI Agents:

Fairness, data protection, sustainability, and human dignity must be core components of every system.

## Human Oversight

"Human-in-the-Loop" approaches—where humans remain involved in critical decisions—are essential.
Major actions, such as high-value financial transactions or identity changes, should not occur without human approval.

## Security Architecture

Decentralized systems must be made more robust against attacks and abuse.

This includes:

- Multi-signature approvals

- Risk analyses

- Regular audits and certifications of AI Agents

## Education and Awareness

Users must understand how AI Agents work, the risks they entail, and how they should be used responsibly. Technical education must not remain an elite discipline—it must become widely accessible across society.

# A deep dive and conclusion

The convergence of AI Agents and Web3 Domain Names represents one of the most intriguing technological intersections of the 21st century. On one side, Web3 domains offer decentralized, user-owned digital identities powered by blockchain. On the other, AI Agents are autonomous, intelligent systems capable of operating independently, making decisions, and learning from complex environments.

Together, these technologies have the potential to revolutionize how we own, manage, and utilize digital assets — but they also introduce significant risks and ethical questions that must be carefully considered.

**Understanding the Concepts**

- Web3 Domains are blockchain-based domain names (such as .eth, .crypto, .nft) that exist independently of traditional registrars like ICANN. They are owned directly by individuals via wallets and can be used for websites, payments, decentralized apps (dApps), and digital identities.

- AI Agents are self-operating programs powered by artificial intelligence, capable of decision-making, learning, and interacting with systems autonomously. They can execute tasks like market analysis, portfolio management, negotiations, and customer support — without human intervention.

When combined, AI Agents can autonomously buy, sell, manage, and optimize Web3 domains at scale, introducing a profound shift in how digital ownership is handled in the decentralized future.

# Advantages of AI Agents in the Web3 Domain Ecosystem

### Automation and Efficiency

AI Agents can automate otherwise tedious and complex tasks related to domain management:

- Real-time monitoring of available blockchain domain names

- Automated domain acquisition based on predictive market trends

- Renewal and security management for domain portfolios

- Intelligent valuation models for buying and selling domains

This reduces human error, increases scalability, and makes domain management accessible even to users without technical expertise.

## Smarter Investment Strategies

The Web3 domain space is emerging as a lucrative investment category.
AI Agents can:

- Analyze blockchain transaction patterns

- Track social media sentiment

- Forecast emerging trends (e.g., upcoming NFT projects, DAO formations)

- Make faster buy/sell decisions than any human trader

This data-driven decision-making could offer early-mover advantages in a volatile market.

## Personalized Identity Management

An AI Agent linked to your Web3 domain could:

- Update your public blockchain profile

- Manage different layers of privacy (selective disclosure of wallet addresses, credentials, etc.)

- Curate decentralized content personalized to the viewer (e.g., a dynamic homepage based on user wallet metadata)

Such smart identity systems could reshape how individuals present themselves online, offering more control and personalization than traditional Web2 platforms.

### 24/7 Operation Across Global Markets

Web3 is inherently global and always-on. AI Agents, unbound by time zones or human limitations, can operate 24/7 to:

- Participate in domain auctions

- Monitor expiry dates

- Negotiate domain leases

- Respond to offers or threats in real time

This uninterrupted operational capacity gives significant strategic advantages.

# Risks and Challenges of AI Agents in Web3 Domains

### Autonomy Risks and "Runaway Agents"

While autonomy is a strength, it is also a liability.
An AI Agent might:

- Misinterpret market data and over-purchase irrelevant domains

- Execute transactions based on outdated, manipulated, or fraudulent inputs

- Develop decision-making patterns that its creators did not anticipate

"Runaway Agents," acting outside intended parameters, could cause financial loss or reputational damage.

## Ethical and Legal Grey Areas

Ownership disputes could arise when AI Agents act:

- Who is legally responsible for an agent's acquisition of a trademarked domain?

- Can an autonomous agent enter a binding smart contract under current legal frameworks?

- How do intellectual property rights apply when AI buys or trades domains linked to brands?

The absence of clear regulations around autonomous digital transactions poses significant compliance and litigation risks.

## Security Vulnerabilities

AI systems operating in a decentralized environment are tempting targets:

- Hackers could inject malicious training data (data poisoning)

- AI Agents could be redirected via smart contract exploits

- Unauthorized parties could hijack AI-controlled wallets or domain registries

Without strong encryption, secure code audits, and proactive monitoring, critical digital assets could be lost or compromised.

## Market Manipulation and Inequality

Advanced AI Agents could create an unfair advantage:

- Wealthier entities could deploy highly sophisticated AI swarms to dominate premium domain markets

- Smaller investors might be priced out, leading to centralization in what should be a decentralized system

- Insider AI systems could collude to fix domain prices, creating artificial scarcity

Without governance frameworks, AI-driven market concentration could erode Web3's promise of democratization.

# Strategic Recommendations for Safe Adoption

To fully realize the potential of AI Agents in Web3 domains while minimizing risks, several principles must be embraced:

- Transparency: All AI decisions (buy, sell, transfer) must be logged on-chain for public auditability.

- Human Oversight: Critical actions (e.g., purchases over a threshold value) should require human approval.

- Ethical AI Design: Responsibility-by-design should be mandated, ensuring that AI respects legal and moral boundaries.

- Robust Security Practices: Mandatory audits, multi-signature wallets, and secure data feeds must become standard.

- Progressive Regulation: Governments and decentralized governance bodies should collaborate to create flexible legal frameworks without stifling innovation.

# Conclusion

The integration of AI Agents and Web3 Domain Names heralds a new era of smart ownership, decentralized identity management, and autonomous investing.
When leveraged responsibly, AI can unlock massive efficiencies and opportunities in the decentralized economy.
However, if left unchecked, the very autonomy that makes AI attractive could also undermine trust, equality, and security in Web3.

Thus, our approach must be cautious but optimistic: combining innovation with oversight, and autonomy with accountability.

The future of Web3 domains won't just be decentralized — it will be intelligent. But only if we make it wisely so.

# 08 CONCLUSION

*"The adoption of Web3 domain names marks a seismic shift towards user sovereignty and digital self-ownership."*

Max Thompson, Blockchain Researcher
at Decentralize Everything Foundation

# Recap of Key Points

In conclusion, Web3 Domains represent a pivotal advancement in the evolution of the Internet, offering a decentralized, censorship-resistant, and user-centric alternative to traditional domain names and centralized web infrastructure. As we navigate the complexities of the digital age, they emerge as a transformative force with profound implications for online interactions, economies, and governance.

At the core lies the principle of decentralization, empowering individuals, communities, and organizations to assert ownership, control, and governance over their digital identities, data and assets. By leveraging blockchain technology, decentralized storage solutions, and cryptographic protocols, Web3 Domains enable users to transcend the limitations of centralized intermediaries, mitigate risks of censorship and surveillance, and reclaim sovereignty over their online presence. It's huge!

The potential impact extends far beyond technical innovation, encompassing the decentralized internet's social, economic, and political dimensions.

From fostering trust, transparency, and inclusivity within communities to enabling economic empowerment, value creation, and digital asset ownership, Web3 Domains redefine the way we interact, transact, and collaborate online.

However, challenges and opportunities abound as we embark on this transformative journey towards a decentralized internet. Key considerations include addressing scalability, usability, and interoperability barriers, fostering ecosystem growth and adoption, and navigating regulatory and legal frameworks in a rapidly evolving landscape.

In this dynamic landscape, collaboration, experimentation, and continuous iteration are essential to realizing the full promise of advancing the decentralized Internet agenda. By harnessing the collective wisdom, creativity, and ingenuity of global communities, we can chart a course toward a more inclusive, and human-centric internet that empowers individuals, strengthens businesses, communities, and fosters innovation for generations to come.

Now it's on us how we'll use it.

# 09 APPENDIX

## Glossary of Terms about Web3 Domain Names

1. Web3: Refers to the next generation of the internet characterized by decentralized, peer-to-peer, and trustless interactions enabled by blockchain technology and decentralized protocols.

2. Web3 Domain Names: Decentralized Domain Names that are registered, owned, and resolved on blockchain networks, providing censorship-resistant and user-owned alternatives to traditional domain names.

3. Blockchain: A distributed ledger technology that stores transactional records across multiple nodes in a decentralized network, ensuring transparency, immutability, and security of data.

4. Decentralized Naming Systems: Systems that enable the registration, ownership, and resolution of domain names using blockchain technology and decentralized protocols, reducing reliance on centralized domain registrars and DNS infrastructure.

5. Ethereum Name Service (ENS): A decentralized naming system built on the Ethereum blockchain that allows users to register and manage domain names ending in .eth, providing human-readable identifiers for Ethereum addresses and decentralized applications (DApps).

6. Handshake: A decentralized naming and certificate authority system that operates on its own blockchain, enabling users to register and manage top-level domain names (TLDs) without relying on centralized domain registries or certificate authorities.

7. Unstoppable Domains: A company that offers Web3 domain registration services on various blockchain networks, allowing users to register and manage domain names ending in .crypto, .bitcoin, not, .x, .zil, and other extensions, providing censorship-resistant and user-owned domain alternatives.

8. Decentralized Identity (DID): A self-sovereign identity framework that enables individuals to create, own, and control their digital identities using decentralized identifiers (DIDs) and verifiable credentials stored on blockchain networks.

9. Non-Fungible Token (NFT): A unique digital asset that represents ownership or proof of authenticity of a specific item or piece of content, such as artwork, collectibles, or domain names, recorded on a blockchain network.

10. InterPlanetary File System (IPFS): A protocol and peer-to-peer network for storing and sharing hypermedia content in a decentralized and distributed manner, providing resilient and censorship-resistant hosting solutions for decentralized websites and applications.

11. Swarm: A decentralized storage and content distribution platform built on the Ethereum blockchain, allowing users to store and retrieve data in a peer-to-

peer network of nodes, providing censorship-resistant and immutable storage solutions.

12. Decentralized Autonomous Organization (DAO): An organization governed by smart contracts and decentralized consensus mechanisms, where members collectively make decisions, manage resources, and govern operations without central authority or intermediaries.

13. Smart Contract: Self-executing contracts with pre-defined rules and conditions encoded on a blockchain network, enabling automated and trustless execution of agreements, transactions, and protocols without intermediaries.

14. Tokenization: The process of converting real-world or digital assets into tokens represented on blockchain networks, allowing for fractional ownership, transferability, and liquidity of assets such as domain names, real estate, or securities.

15. Decentralized Finance (DeFi): A financial ecosystem built on blockchain networks that aim to democratize access to financial services, products, and infrastructure, enabling peer-to-peer lending, borrowing, trading, and asset management without traditional intermediaries.

# 10 DISCLAIMER

## Affiliate Disclosure

StakedX participates in various affiliate marketing programs, which means StakedX may get paid commissions on purchases or signups made through our links to other sites.

# Disclaimer

RISK DISCLAIMER: This ebook includes information about cryptocurrencies and other financial instruments and about brokers, exchanges, and other entities trading such instruments. Both cryptocurrencies and CFDs are complex instruments and come with a high risk of losing money. You should carefully consider whether you understand how these instruments work and whether you can afford to take the high risk of losing your money. StakedX encourages you to perform your own research before making any investment decision and to avoid investing in any financial instrument which you do not fully understand how it works and what are the risks involved.